The New Nationalism
How the Populist Right is Defeating Globalism and Awakening a New Political Order

Stephen R. Turley, Ph.D.

TURLEY TALKS
A New Conservative Age is Rising
www.TurleyTalks.com

ISBN-13:978-1727351590

ISBN-10:1727351592

Table of Contents

The New Nationalism

All over the world, a nationalist revolution is underway. In the past 17 years, the actual number of nationalist and populist parties across the European continent has nearly doubled, growing from 33 to 63.[1] And these parties are seeing extraordinary electoral success. The share of votes won by populist parties in Europe has tripled in the course of such time, from 8.5 percent of the European vote to nearly 25 percent. Since the spring of 2010, there have been over a dozen Parliamentary elections throughout Western Europe, and we can see the electoral surge of nationalist populist parties throughout these elections. In March of 2017, Geert Wilder's Dutch Freedom Party came in second place, a marked difference from 2006 when they came in fifth place. We've seen a comparable surge with the Flemish nationalist and secessionist party in Belgian parliamentary elections, along with the rise of the Swedish Democrats and the anti-European party the True Finns. Marine Le Pen doubled the support of National Front in her recent presidential campaign against the centrist Macron. In Italy, the once fringe Northern League has entered into a

---

[1] https://institute.global/insight/renewing-centre/european-populism-trends-threats-and-future-prospects.

coalition government with the populist Five Star Movement. The so-called Visegrád Four – Hungary, Poland, Slovakia, and the Czech Republic – all have nationalist governments hostile to the EU's immigration quotas, a hostility bolstered of late by Austria's electoral turn to the right and the rise of the far-right party Alternative for Germany in their latest rounds of elections.

In the most recent year of elections to date, 2017, the center-left all but collapsed throughout Europe. A total of 946 districts held political elections that year, and the center-left coalitions held their own or improved in a mere 56 districts, or just under six percent of European elections. According to *The Guardian*'s analysis, in almost 94 percent of districts, the center-left lost out to center-right, nationalist or so-called far-right parties, as well as populist left parties, which were often as hostile to the Eurozone as the far-right.[2] *The New York Times*' assessment was nothing short of dire: "In most major Western European countries, centre-left parties are in retreat, and in some cases they have practically ceased to exist."[3]

But if we widen our lens, we can see that Europe is hardly exceptional in this nationalist rebellion. In its Eurasian context, Russia has drawn inspiration of late from a resurgent neo-Byzantium sentiment, what U.S. Naval War College professor John R. Schindler calls a "Third Rome"

---

[2] https://www.theguardian.com/politics/ng-interactive/2017/dec/29/2017-and-the-curious-demise-of-europes-centre-left.

[3] https://www.nytimes.com/2017/12/28/opinion/germany-social-democrats-coalition.html.

ideology, which involves "a powerful admixture of Orthodoxy, ethnic mysticism, and Slavophile tendencies that has deep resonance in Russian history."[4] It's neighbor Turkey, under the leadership of Recep Tayyip Erdoğan, is more and more turning away from its Kemalist secularism and returning to its Ottoman roots. The religious nationalist Bharatiya Janata Party has been increasingly implementing Hindutva, something akin to a Hindu version of Sharia law, throughout India. Mongolia has recently voted in a nationalist populist president. Imperial Shintoism is more popular today at the highest levels of the Japanese government than it has been since World War II. Samoa just altered its constitution, formally declaring itself a Christian nation. Bermuda has recently voted to reverse their Supreme Court's legalization of same-sex marriage. Latin American nations such as Columbia, Chile, and Peru have all turned to the political right. And of course, in the United States, Donald Trump was elected president after campaigning on a nationalist populist 'America First' platform.

There is no question that a mass wave of rightwing nationalism is sweeping the globe. But why? What is happening here? Is all of this a coincidence, or are there clear, discernible trends that are operative in all of these examples? And what does it mean for the future of the globalist world system? Could these national examples be more than just isolated incidents within their respective

---

[4] John R. Schindler, "Putinism and the Anti-WEIRD Coalition," http://20committee.com/2014/04/07/putinism-and-the-anti-weird-coalition/.

continents, or are they indicative of a new political order rising in our midst?

This book seeks to answer precisely these questions. I will argue that nationalist movements throughout the world exemplify common political trends and cultural currents that indicate we are most certainly on the cusp of a worldwide political paradigm shift; the globalist political and economic order so dominant over the last several decades is in fact collapsing under the weight of a renewed sense of nationalism, populism, and traditionalism that is awakening nothing less than a new political order throughout the world.

What's *New* About the New Nationalism

Of course, proponents of the secular globalist liberal order hardly welcome this paradigm shift; indeed, they see nothing *new* about what I'm calling here the New Nationalism and its emerging political order. It's become rather fashionable among leftwing activists and media outlets to denounce the rise of the new right as little more than reheated fascism and Nazism. Since the election of Donald Trump, we've seen the advent of ANTIFA or 'anti-fascist' groups ironically employing intimidating and totalitarian tendencies to shut down ideas and speakers they don't like. In fact, while researching for this book on a university library database, my search for the keyword 'fascism' elicited as its first option: 'fascism and Donald Trump.' The British journalist John Lichfield observed that the French National Front Leader Marine Le Pen's attempt to rebrand her party actually cast it further into fascist territory. Specifically, Le Pen's blend of nationalism and socialism has, in Lichfield's words, "a dark history," such that the new National Front "is more authentically fascist" than it was before the rebranding.[5] The ultra-liberal Chris Hedges wrote what some have called a "call to arms" against the efforts of the likes of Pat Robertson and Jerry Falwell to turn America into a Christian nation, aptly and not-so-subtly titled *American Fascists: The Christian Right and the War on America.*

And yet, what eludes these rather pernicious pejorative-laced assessments of the emerging nationalist movements around the world are the various ways in which the current political right is a rejection of the philosophical commitments so foundational to fascism and Nazism. Scholars such as Roger Griffen see the key characteristic of fascism as what he calls *palingenesis*, the notion of a totalitarian-led national rebirth through the overthrow of a supposedly oppressive world political and cultural order. For fascists during the interwar period, such a world order involved the fear and threat of the spread of worldwide communism. The global conquest of totalitarian fascism was justified in light of such a threat, since fascism was thought to provide the necessary bulwark against the onslaught of global Marxism on the one hand and the perpetuation, indeed, the rebirth of a population's cultural integrity on the other. For the Nazis in particular, palingenesis included the extensive reliance on modern forms of biological eugenic engineering at the service of both anti-communist and anti-Semitic sentiments.

---

[5] John Lichfield, "Why we should be scared of Marine le Pen's Front National," *Independent,* December 8, 2015.

However, for what I'm calling here the New Nationalism, the communist threat is of course gone, as is any notion of biological racial superiority. In terms of anti-Semitism, not only are many of the cotemporary nationalist right's leaders pro-Israel, but the nation of Israel with its rightwing government is one of the starkest examples of the New Nationalism! It would certainly be rather odd to plausibly refer to Israel as fascist and its government neo-Nazi. Yes, the New Nationalists are hostile to the current globalist world order, but they have no interest in or rationale for any kind of worldwide conquest, but instead seek to restore the integrity of their national borders and sovereignty. They affirm the dignity of democracy and, in the case of Europe, see themselves as in fact fighting for the restoration of democratic integrity in their own nations as over against the perceived totalitarian tendencies from the 'Bullies in Brussels.' It is no wonder, then, as Nigel Copsey has pointed out, scholars of the contemporary nationalist right or far-right in Europe have in fact formed a consensus opinion that such parties are emphatically *not* fascist but represent rather a new chapter in the history of rightwing politics.[6]

Having said that, it is true that the racial politics of the so-called Alt-Right in the United States as well as neo-fascists in Europe are attracted to and/or aligned with the New Nationalism. However, we need not commit the fallacy of inferring that the New Nationalism is itself neo-fascist; instead, we need to inquire into the common belief system,

---

[6] Nigel Copsey, "The Radical Right and Fascism," in Jens Rydgren (ed.), *The Oxford Handbook of the Radical Right* (Oxford: Oxford University Press, 2018), 118.

sentiment, or orientation shared by those on the nationalist right.[7] The key sentiments shared by all on the nationalist right is the rejection of the anti-cultural processes of globalization and its secular aristocracy on the one hand, and the restoration of the integrity of the nation-state and the reaffirmation of its shared culture, customs, and traditions on the other. While neo-fascists are in fact attracted and agreeable to such beliefs and sentiments, the beliefs and sentiments themselves, for the reasons stated above, are not neo-fascist.

Defining Nationalism

The term *nationalism* is derived from the Latin term *natio*, which refers to a place of birth, as indicated by the term *nativity*. This is actually the root of the English term *nation*, which eventually became associated with a people group occupying a homeland – a common place of birth – and from there the term *nation* developed a cultural connotation, referring to a people group who share a common history, religion, and overall vision of life, as well as a common economy and political order for all its members. Nationalism can thus be construed as a collective commitment that seeks the well-being of all of these factors, seeking the protection and perpetuation of a common homeland wherein a common culture, economy, and political order flourishes.[8]

---

[7] Copsey, "The Radical Right," 117.
[8] See, for example, Anthony D. Smith, *Nationalism: Theory, Ideology, History* (Malden, MA: Polity Press, 2010).

And so, in these respects, nationalism can be conceived as primarily about maintaining and protecting the political, social, and cultural context by which we forge a sense of what it means to be human, albeit in a nation-state context. And if that's the case, then this return to nation, culture, and tradition that we are seeing throughout the world is simply a return to what is most natural when it comes to our very humanity.

Mass Immigration: The Globalist Threat to the Nation-State

The New Nationalists are united against *globalism*, a vast interlocking mechanism of technology and telecommunications that creates a single worldwide economic and political system.[9] Because globalization eclipses the nation-state with wider transnational economic and political processes, many scholars believe that globalization is bringing an end to the whole concept of distinct nations. Such a dire prospect is not lost on populations, as it is most explicitly exemplified in mass unfettered immigration. As Paul Harris has observed, the porous borders which serve to expedite flows of goods within a globalized economy entail a significant increase in levels of immigration, both legal and illegal.[10] This immigration flow trends along the direction of economic activity: Turks flow into Germany, Albanians ebb into

---

[9] See, for example, Anthony Giddens, *Runaway World: How Globalization is Reshaping our Lives* (New York: Routledge, 2000).
[10] Paul A. Harris, "Immigration, Globalization and National Security: An Emerging Challenge to the Modern Administrative State," http://unpan1.un.org/intradoc/groups/public/documents/aspa/unpan0 06351.pdf.

Greece, North Africans into France, Pakistanis into England, and Mexicans into the U.S.[11]

Increasingly, the world feels like it is flattening, with one nation in effect blending into the other. As such, the cultural uniqueness so indispensable to the perpetuation of national identities appears to be withering worldwide, with a globalist, monolithic, consumer-based culture taking over. Globalism has thus provoked a worldwide backlash, where populations are turning more and more toward their own culture, customs, and traditions, and reasserting their national sovereignty and border security as over against what they perceive as the anti-cultural processes of globalization and its secular aristocracy.

Populism: The Electoral Support for the New Nationalism

In the midst of this globalist threat to national sovereignty and identity, it is no wonder that the New Nationalism is emerging as a radically *populist* phenomenon. The term *populism* is notoriously difficult to define, but for our purposes, I use the term as a shorthand to refer to movements that have a certain set of characteristics.[12] Populism involves (1) a rejection of elites in favor of "the people"; (2) a rejection of internationalism in favor of a commitment to national interests, an 'America First' kind

---

[11] Victor Davis Hanson, "The Global Immigration Problem," http://www.realclearpolitics.com/articles/2007/05/the_global_immigration_problem.html.

[12] Douglas J. Elliott, "Financial Institutions in an Age of Populism," http://www.oliverwyman.com/content/dam/oliver-wyman/v2/publications/2017/mar/Financial-Institutions-in-an-Age-of-Populism.pdf.

of approach to things; (3) a rejection of elite institutions, which are viewed as broken or rigged; (4) a scorn for experts and the embracing of 'common sense'; and (5) a desire for a strong leader to drive change. So negatively, populism involves a rejection of elites, a rejection of internationalism, a rejection of elite institutions, and a rejection of elitist experts. Positively, populism involves affirming the common man and the cultural landscape and traditions of a nation's heartland, the affirmation of one's own nation over all others first and foremost, an affirmation of common sense, and the support of a strong leader to drive change.

The New Nationalism is perfectly postured for populist appeal. Globalist inspired multiculturalism by its very nature turns nations on their heads when it comes to immigration. Instead of immigrants learning to accommodate themselves to the culture to which they've emigrated, which is what they've been doing for thousands of years, the host-culture is now forced to accommodate itself to the immigrants. Rather than assimilate into the majority culture, native populations are forced to accommodate themselves to the migrants. This is what leaders of the National Front in France often say: "Is it France that has to adapt her principles for the immigrants or is it the immigrants who must adapt their customs to the rules of this country?"

And so, leaders in the New Nationalism promote themselves as defenders of the people, the voice of the citizens that stand up against the globalist elite who advocate solely for the migrant at the expense of the customs, culture, and traditions of the host nation.[13] The New Nationalist parties are thus thoroughly populist; they speak the language of the people and are at war, as it were, with the globalist elite; they're characterized by a marked anti-establishment rhetoric, are strongly opposed to the European Union, and are of course a nightmare for Brussels.

The New Nationalism and Retraditionalization

A final feature of the New Nationalism is an intentional resistance against the secularizing dynamics of globalism. Built into globalization processes is what scholars call *detraditionalization,* or various mechanisms by which local customs and traditions are relativized to wider economic, scientific, and technocratic forces.[14] Once social life is caught up in a global industrialized economic system, it is propelled away from traditional, national, and local practices and beliefs.

And so, globalization involves a predictable counter reaction at the local and national level aptly termed *retraditionalization,* which involves a renewed interest in "traditions of wisdom that have proved their validity through the test of history," or "a longing for spiritual traditions and practices that have stood the test of time, and therefore can be valued as authentic resources for spiritual renewal."[15] As we shall see in a number of our case

---

[13] Hans-Georg Betz, "The Radical Right and Populism," in Jens Rydgren (ed.), *The Oxford Handbook of the Radical Right* (Oxford: Oxford University Press, 2018), 97.

[14] Giddens, *Runaway World*, 61-65, 91.

[15] Leif Gunnar Engedal, "*Homo Viator.* The Search for Identity and Authentic Spirituality in a Post-modern Context," in Kirsi Tirri (ed.) *Religion, Spirituality and Identity* (Bern: Peter Lang, 2006), 45-64, 58.

studies below, retraditionalization is not limited simply to spiritual renewal or religious revival; it often involves a reconfiguration of political, cultural, and educational norms around pre-modern religious beliefs and practices as a response to the secularizing processes of globalization.[16]

The New Nationalism is thus, in many parts of the world, a distinctively *religious* nationalism. Indeed, sociologist Rodney Stark argues that we are currently in the midst of the single greatest religious surge the world has ever seen.[17] According to the authors of *God's Century,* traditional religions throughout the world "enjoy *greater capacity for political influence today than at any time in modern history – and perhaps ever.*"[18] It is thus not a coincidence that Donald Trump's first international trip as president, where he visited Jerusalem, Riyadh, and Rome, was framed explicitly as a world tour of the Abrahamic religions. Vice President Mike Pence has visited Franklin Graham's summit on international religious freedom and the annual meeting of Christians United for Israel. And as Emma Green of The Atlantic has noted, religion and religious groups were instrumental in one of the year's biggest foreign-policy moves, which was President Trump's decision to

---

[16] Ivan Varga, "Detraditionalization and Retraditionalization," in Mark Juergensmeyer and Wade Clark Roof (eds.), *Encyclopedia of Global Religion* (Los Angeles: Sage Publications, 2012), 295-98, 297.

[17] Rodney Stark, *The Triumph of Faith: Why the World is More Religious than Ever* (Wilmington, DE: ISI Books, 2015).

[18] Monica Duffy Toft, Daniel Philpott, Timothy Samuel Shah, *God's Century: Resurgent Religion and Global Politics* (New York: Norton and Company, 2011), 49, emphasis original.

relocate the American embassy in Israel from Tel Aviv to Jerusalem.[19]

In what follows, we will be exploring a number of case studies reflective of these nationalist, populist, and traditionalist trends. In so doing, I hope to demonstrate that though each nation involves its own unique political and cultural context, there are nevertheless discernible patterns that transcend the specific national contexts. These common currents of renewed nationalist, populist, and traditionalist sentiments are indeed sweeping across the world, effectively defeating globalism and awakening a new political order.

---

[19] Emma Green, "How Religion Made a Global Comeback in 2017," https://www.theatlantic.com/international/archive/2017/12/religion-trump/548780/.

CHAPTER 1

Hungary: A Renewed Christian Democracy

It was April 8th, 2018. Hungarian Prime Minister Viktor Orban and his Fidesz Party alliance were going for their third straight term in power. This was an absolutely crucial election for the globalists and the nationalists of Europe; indeed, some called it the 'Battle of Budapest.' European Union supporters such as far-left billionaire George Soros pumped millions of dollars into this election, with ad campaigns trying to galvanize the youth of Hungary to rise up against their 'racist' and 'homophobic' prime minister, lest their nation slide into a xenophobic dictatorship. But to no avail; the wave of nationalist-inspired anti-immigrant, pro-culture, pro-tradition sentiment that has flooded Europe prevailed in Hungary. Viktor Orban and his Fidesz Party won a massive landslide, winning 134 seats in a 199-seat parliament, a super-majority which allows Fidesz to actually alter Hungary's constitution if they so choose.

Shortly after his re-election, Viktor Orban announced his vision to build what he calls a 'Christian democracy.' In an interview with Kossuth Radio, the prime minister outlined his political agenda for the following four years, solidifying the making of a Christian democracy. Having read through a number of Orban's interviews and speeches, I've identified four major distinctives that characterize what he calls a 'Christian democracy,' and I see these operative not just in Hungary, but indeed in other nations such as Poland, Russia, and the Republic of Georgia as well. Thus, this outline will help not only better understand what is going on in modern Hungary, but it will also give us a better sense of what the New Nationalist reawakening of a vibrant European civilization entails.

Separation of Powers, Not Purpose

First, we need to address the whole notion that a Christian democracy means a theocracy. This is probably the most common objection coming from the corporatist globalists in Brussels and in Berlin, that Orban wants to create an authoritarian theocracy. In fact, nothing can be farther from the truth. As Orban makes clear, Christian democracies absolutely affirm a separation of powers between church and state. The church and the state are wholly unique and distinctive institutions. But what makes Christian democracies different from globalist societies is that while they recognize a separation of powers between church and state, *they don't recognize a separation of purpose.* The church and state are two very different institutions, but both serve a common end or goal, which is to honor, celebrate, and preserve the nation's culture, customs, and traditions rooted in Christian and classical civilization. This is in no way, shape, or form a theocracy where nations are ruled by the church or by a council of religious leaders or anything even remotely like that. Orban's vision of a Christian democracy is about the church and state working together to protect and to perpetuate the traditions, customs, and culture of a nation in light of the unique threats posed by the anti-cultural, anti-traditional, anti-national processes of globalization and its secular aristocracy. Church and state operate within their own respective spheres of authority, but these spheres cooperate and work together to protect and promote the culture, customs, and traditions that define the collective identity of a nation rooted in a distinctively Christian vision of life.

Protecting Borders, Protecting Values

The second key distinctive is the protection of national borders. Prime Minister Orban made this distinctive a top priority in the last election. In a Christian democracy, what we have to understand is that if the protection of a nation's culture, customs, and traditions is paramount to the role of church and state, there's going to have to be a concerted effort to protect the borders of that culture, custom, and tradition. This is because when borders are opened akin to the way the EU is insisting its member nations open them, *inevitably these open borders translate into open values.*

Cultural anthropologists like Mary Douglas have developed the critical connection between borders and bodies in human culture. For example, have you ever noticed that if there are restrictions as to whom you can get married in a population, like among Jews for example, that such restrictions actually end up reflecting restrictions on who can or can't enter into your society? If one is not allowed to marry someone from another group, those groups tend not to mix with one another. The boundaries for our bodies tend to reflect the wider boundaries of the group to which we belong. The do's and don't's regulating national boundaries are lived out personally via the moral codes inscribed on individual bodies. Thus, if anyone can enter into your country, well then by definition you can marry anyone. If there are no restrictions at your national border, there will be a comparable absence of restrictions in your personal and moral order.

So, if these cultural anthropologists are correct, and I most certainly believe that they are, then there is a plausible cultural sense that *open borders mean open values.* And so, what does this mean for the EU's immigration quotas? Very simply, mass unfettered immigration fulfills the political precondition for more liberal democratic social policies. The less secure a nation's borders, the less secure a nation's customs and culture. Orban's vision of a Christian democracy thus sees border protection and immigration enforcement as the necessary precondition for the protection and perpetuation of Christian values and identity.

Economic Nationalism

A third key distinctive of Christian democracy is what is called 'economic nationalism.' This is perhaps the most misunderstood element of Christian democracy, in that economic nationalism is often associated merely with protectionism and the imposition of tariffs on all foreign imports. However, as scholars have noted, the problem with this equivocation of economic nationalism as mere protectionism is that there's simply no nation or nationalism in this equivocation.[20] Said differently, critics often wrongly leave out the *nationalist* dimension when they reduce economic nationalism to protectionism. What they're actually doing is confusing nationalism with *statism*; while protectionism certainly involves the state imposing tariffs on certain goods or regulating what can be bought and sold, state activity is not necessarily *nationalist*. There are very important differences between statism and nationalism: statism involves institutional activity while nationalism involves trans-institutional phenomena such as community, culture, custom, language, religion, and ethnicity. Statism is institutional while nationalism is trans-institutional.

And so, the important point here, is that while economic nationalism may involve protectionism, it can't be reduced to protectionism. Instead, as the name implies, scholars see economic nationalism as an economic approach that is intentionally pursued for the benefit of the culture, custom, and tradition that collectively comprise the nation. Economic nationalism is a facet of national identity, where certain kinds of cultures, traditions, religions, and ethnicities forge distinctive economic policies in accordance with specific national traits. What this means is that economic nationalism can certainly involve protectionist measures, but it can also involve free-trade measures, or subsidies, or controlled markets, or free markets; indeed, economic nationalism can actually be all of the above! It can be very libertarian in some national

---

[20] Eric Helleiner and Andreas Pickel (eds.), *Economic Nationalism in a Globalizing Word* (Ithaca and London: Cornell University Press, 2005).

contexts and highly regulatory in others; the important point here is that the purpose of the economy is for the protection and perpetuation of a nation's culture, customs, and traditions, not the other way around. The economy is not seen as sovereign in an economic nationalist view; the economy is not some scientifically rationalist system that's superimposed on nations and cultures, which in turn ends up belittling and relativizing their customs, religions, and traditions. Instead, the economy here is rightly seen as an extension of national and religious identity; thus, economic nationalism is an important distinctive of a Christian democracy.

The Traditional Family as Society's Foundation

A fourth distinctive is that unlike liberal democracies, the traditional family is supported and protected in Christian democracies. This appears to be a very important distinctive developing in Christian democracies around the world that have been suffering significant demographic decline, but through implementing pro-family measures, these nations have been able to effectively reverse demographic deficits. We're seeing concerted efforts to revitalize the traditional family in Orthodox nations such as Russia and Georgia, as well as in Catholic nations such as Poland. And they've all been very successful in reversing decades of demographic decline. For example, the Republic of Georgia for a number of years has had one of the lowest birthrates in Eastern Europe. And so, the Orthodox Patriarch there, Ilia II, began a campaign where he promised to personally baptize the third or higher child of married Orthodox couples. You had to have had at least two or more children, and then he would personally baptize them. This was back in 2008, and since then, to the astonishment of demographers, Georgia has gone from having one of the lowest birthrates in Eastern Europe to now actually one of the highest. We're seeing a comparable demographic reversal going on in Russia and in Poland.

Of course, without a flourishing, ever expanding demography, a nation becomes inevitably dependent on immigration for funding its entitlements and social welfare programs, which in turn ends up eventually destroying its distinctive customs and traditions. This is exactly what's been going on throughout the EU member nations, most of which are going through a severe demographic deficit. Scholars such as Eric Kaufmann have noticed a correlation between secular notions of life and falling birth rates.[21] In short, we're finding that secular globalist societies don't reproduce; they certainly celebrate abortion, same-sex marriage, and feminism, but, as it turns out, these lifestyle values really are nothing more than civilizational suicide. By contrast, Christian democratic societies celebrate the traditional family, and see it as the foundation for a stable, moral, and flourishing society. And Viktor Orban has committed himself to just such a demographic revitalization in Hungary, and as we saw above, he's not alone.

So, these are the four distinctives of a newly emerging Christian civilization within Europe. Christian democracies

---

[21] Eric Kaufmann, *Shall the Religious Inherit the Earth? Demography and Politics in the Twenty-First Century* (London: Profile Books, 2010).

are characterized by a separation of powers but not a separation of purpose; they are committed to protecting their nations' borders so as to protect their values; they're characterized by a diverse application of economic nationalism as the economy is an extension of national identity; and they're committed to fostering and furthering the natural family for a flourishing future. That's the vision of Christian democracies which is leading Europe and increasingly Western Civilization as a whole into the twenty-first-century and beyond.

CHAPTER 2

Poland vs. The European Union: A New Kind of Leadership

Few nations have stood up to the anti-cultural globalist policies of the European Union like Poland of late. Led by the Law and Justice Party, who won a sweeping victory in their national elections a couple of years back, Poland is experiencing nothing less than a national renaissance, a cultural blossoming that was publicly acknowledged and celebrated by President Donald Trump in his formal state visit to Poland back in July of 2017.

However, Poland has no shortage of detractors, particularly in Brussels. One critic accused Poland of "abdicating" its leading role in Central Europe by refusing to bend to the EU's demands on migrant quotas and internal judicial reforms. But in the process of making these observations, she ended up admitting that the nation of Poland poses a greater existential threat to the EU than does Brexit.[22]

The EU official's name was Elżbieta Bieńkowska, who is herself Polish. She was appointed a Eurocrat by Donald

---

[22] https://www.express.co.uk/news/world/862981/Poland-EU-latest-news-Brexit-news-judicial-reforms-PiS-El-bieta-Bie-kowsk.

Tusk, the current President of the European Council but was also the former prime-minister of Poland, before his centrist globalist Civic Platform Party was swept out of office by the current nationalist populist ruling party, Law and Justice, in a landslide election defeat. She said at an EU Forum taking place in Poland that her nation, in refusing to accept the immigration quotas and judicial restraints and reforms imposed by the EU, has in effect abdicated its role as leader of Central Europe, and that it will take a very long time to rebuild its leadership position, if that were even possible at this point.

Strong words, for sure. But the EU is hardly interested in just words. Brussels has actually called for implementing what's called Article 7 of the EU charter, which would strip Poland of its voting rights in the European Parliament, something that has never been done before to a member nation. However, Bieńkowska argued that the EU had to be very careful with such threats, because Europe is currently going through what she calls a "rightwing crisis," and it is this crisis, she believes, that has the potential to overwhelm the stability and unity of the EU even more than the successful Brexit referendum.

Poland's supposed right wing crisis continues to be denounced by many within our Western elite. Take for example the rather visceral reactions to Poland's annual Independence Day march, held every year on November the 11th to commemorate the anniversary of the restoration of Poland's sovereignty in 1918 from the German, Austrian, and Russian Empires. In response to the latest march where tens of thousands gathered in celebration, here's what a former staffer for Hillary Clinton, Jesse Lehrich, posted on his twitter account: "60,000 Nazis marched on Warsaw." But this slander pales in comparison to the European Parliament, which denounced the march as part of the EU's process to officially censor Poland and strip them of their voting rights. The European Parliament drafted a resolution where Poland's Law and Justice Party has been denounced for allowing "racism, xenophobia and neo-fascism on Poland's streets," which turns out to have been language crafted by an unnamed member of Poland's chief opposition party in the European Parliament, a fact that drew a very sharp rebuke from Beata Szydło, the then prime-minister of Poland.

With all this in mind, I can't help but wonder whether Bieńkowska's twin-fold concern reveals something far deeper than merely a loss of leadership position and a rightwing crisis. It would seem to be the case that such concerns reveal a far greater concern among Eurocrats and our globalist elite: perhaps Poland *is* exercising extraordinary leadership*, but the kind that poses the greatest threat to the stability and perpetuity of the EU.* Of course, Poland is a major leader among European nations today; this was formally recognized by the state visit of President Donald Trump. We may therefore interpret this whole notion of a 'rightwing crisis' as nothing less than Europe experiencing the rise of a new leadership, a new democratic vision of the world that sees nation, culture, custom, tradition, religion, language and land as central to what it means to be human. More and more Europeans no longer want a world-order predicated on laws, protocols, and bureaucratic procedures that govern the world through unelected elites in a one-size-fits-all standardization that marginalizes all borders, cultures, traditions, customs, and ethnicities to wider transnational economic concerns. Europeans increasingly want their continent back, replete with its distinct identities and ethnicities who are all united in their unique expressions of a single classical and Christian faith, that very faith that the EU refuses to recognize as an intrinsic component to its governance.

Hence, as far as the EU is concerned, it doesn't care about what religion this sea of refugees that's flooding the continent represents; but I'll tell you who does, and that's the Polish people. Perhaps you heard of the thousands of Polish Catholics who recently formed human chains on the country's borders, praying that God would save Poland, Europe, and the world from an Islamization that they see as the inevitable consequence of a Brussels-mandated open borders immigration policy. They recited their rosaries together as a mass spiritual force, and they were lined up along the 2,200-mile border with Germany, the Czech Republic, Slovakia, Ukraine, Belarus, Lithuania, Russia and the Baltic Sea. And even people in boats joined the event, to help form chains across Polish rivers.[23] During the mass that was held and that was broadcast live on television, the archbishop of Krakow called on believers to pray "for the other European nations to make them understand, that it is necessary to return to their Christian roots so that Europe would remain Europe."[24]

---

[23] https://www.pri.org/stories/2017-10-07/polish-catholics-come-together-countrys-borders-praying-save-poland
[24] Ibid.

Indeed, this has been the consistent position of prime minister Mateusz Morawiecki, who has stated that the goal of Poland is to see what he called the re-Christianization of Europe. For Poland, there is simply no future for Europe apart from its Christian heritage and tradition. In a recent interview, Morawiecki was quick to contrast the richness and beauty of Polish culture and traditions with the EU's secular, sterile, and corporation-based transcultural, transnational values that are all too often hostile to historic Christian tradition and custom.[25] Morawiecki said that the EU's secular values are in effect stripping Europe of the very cultural and traditional foundations that have made Europe such an astonishing human civilization and without which, Europe really has no discernibly European future. By contrast, he cited Poland as an example of a European nation that seeks to revive and draw from its Christian history and foundation as the firm basis by which its people can prosper and flourish in the future.

Morawiecki pointed to the recent reversal in Poland's alarming demographic decline that up until this point plagued the population for the last several years. In just the last two years, Poland has gone from one of the lowest birth rates in Europe to one of the highest; they were in twentieth place among European repopulation statistics in 2015; today, as of 2018, they are ranked fourth, just behind France, Hungary, and Austria. And notice, three of those four nations today have rightwing, conservative, and pro-Christian governments.

---

[25] https://www.lifesitenews.com/news/new-polish-pm-sees-return-to-christian-roots-as-only-way-to-stop-europes-de.

All of this raises an important question: Is this not leadership? Are massive prayer groups organized together throughout the nation in order to ask God's blessings on Poland and all the nations of Europe considered examples of extraordinary leadership? Isn't Morawiecki's vision of a renewed Christian civilization as evidenced by Poland's demographic reversal a mark of true leadership?

Well, the answer to this is rather simple: No, not if you're the EU, which sees prayer gatherings and the like as nothing more than a political stunt, an act of stagecraft designed to insight racism, Islamophobia and xenophobia. This isn't the leadership that Eurocrats advocate, and in fact, they believe it's the very opposite of the kind of leadership that Europe and the world needs. The kind of leadership Europe needs is for Poland to take in its share of mandated immigrants from predominantly Islamic territories and show the rest of the world what a commitment to EU values really looks like.

However, Jarosław Kaczyński, the leader of the ruling nationalist Law and Justice Party, remains undaunted. He recently said that the burden of dealing with the current migrant crisis in Europe should fall on those countries which actually encouraged the influx, such as Germany, rather than those who opposed it.[26] Kaczyński has said Poland will take part in the EU program for refugees, because they are a Christian people who are going to come to the aid of those in need; however, what Poland refuses to do is expose their nation to the same cultural, demographic,

---

[26] https://www.breitbart.com/london/2017/05/22/germany-created-migrant-crisis-pay-consequences/.

and economic catastrophes that the rest of Western Europe has opened itself up to. There is no reason for the Polish people to radically lower their living standards and quality of life, as well as negate their unique customs, traditions, and way of life to meet the EU's one-size-fits-all standardized secularized globalized demands. Thus Kaczyński argues that the nation of Poland has a full moral right to say an emphatic 'No!' to the globalist polices mandated by the elite in Brussels.

Thus, Poland is standing up to the EU, they are asserting their sovereignty, their faith, their Christianity, their culture, and their people as worthy of protection. And in so doing, they are helping to ignite a nationalist fire throughout the whole of Europe. And as that fire sets ablaze, it may most certainly turn out that the greatest threat to the unity and stability of the EU was not the Brexit or even the current immigration and economic crises; rather, the greatest threat to the unity and stability of the EU is none other than the prayers, the customs and, yes, the leadership of Poland itself.

CHAPTER 3

Bulgaria: Border Security without Euroskepticism

On June 28 and 29 of 2018, a European Summit of the heads of state of the various nations in the European Union gathered together to try to avert the collapse of German Chancellor Angela Merkel's increasingly brittle coalition. A couple of weeks prior to the Summit, Horst Seehofer, Merkel's own interior minister and head of her key coalition partner the Christian Social Union in Bavaria, basically gave Merkel an ultimatum: either get rid of this fresh crop of migrants and refugees from Bavarian borders or they will go ahead and work with Austria to secure the borders without her. The former option contradicted Merkel's refugee policy, while the latter option would require Merkel to fire her interior minister and thereby lose the support of the CSU, hence collapsing her coalition. And so, an emergency European Summit was scheduled to try to find other nations that would be willing to take in the migrants and refugees and salvage what's left of Merkel's political credibility.

Unfortunately for Merkel, nations like the Visegrad Four – Hungary, Poland, the Czech Republic, and Slovakia – along with Austria, Italy, and the Nordic nations such as Denmark and Sweden, made it clear that they weren't going to have anything to do with taking in these migrants and refugees, let alone agree to anything even remotely resembling immigration quotas as mandated from Brussels.

One nation in particular showed itself to be particularly dedicated to border control and national sovereignty: Bulgaria. In fact, the prime minister of Bulgaria, Boyko Borissov, came out of that meeting calling for a very simple solution to the entire migrant crisis in Europe: [1] close the borders, [2] detain illegal immigrants who made it past the borders, and [3] deport them back to their country of origin.[27] One reason why Borissov spoke out so forcefully was because Bulgaria is disproportionately affected by what is known as the Dublin Regulation, a protocol that sends immigrants and refugees back to the European state where they first crossed the border, and that means more times than not nations like Bulgaria, along with Greece and Italy. The Dublin Regulation was floated as a possible solution for Merkel, and so the prime minister of Bulgaria felt he needed to make it absolutely clear that Bulgaria would not accept any such plan.

What has happened politically in Bulgaria is becoming almost par for the course in European politics. Bulgaria is one of the European nations that's recently turned to the nationalist right. In November of 2016, just a week after Donald Trump was elected president of the United States, Bulgaria elected their own nationalist populist as president

---

[27] http://www.balkaninsight.com/en/article/bulgaria-s-pm-urges-the-closure-of-external-eu-borders-to-tackle-migration-06-18-2018.

of their nation. And then, in March of 2017, the conservative rightist GERB party (the initials stand for 'coat of arms') won their national elections, along with a coalition of so-called 'far-right' parties that formed an alliance called the United Patriots. And so, there was no way that Bulgaria was going to even remotely be an ally with Merkel and her quest for globalist-inspired open borders.

That said, what is of interest is how the New Nationalism in Eastern Europe differs from that of Western Europe. The Bulgarian nationalist right, like the other nationalist right parties in Eastern Europe, is not Euroskeptic or anti-EU. Scholars have noticed that one of the interesting differences between the nationalist right in Eastern Europe and the nationalist right in Western Europe is that the Eastern European parties, the so-called 'far-right' parties, generally do not share the intense Euroskepticism of the nationalist right in Western Europe. For example, none of the nationalist right parties in Eastern Europe is calling for a referendum or a petition to exit the EU akin to what we saw with Brexit or current talks of Frexit in France or Swexit in Sweden. One of the major reasons for this is the fall of the Berlin wall and the whole notion that national sovereignty for nations formerly behind the Iron Curtain became quickly associated with alliances with the West, and particularly with Brussels. Simply put, alliances with Western Europe and Western European institutions meant freedom from Soviet rule. The whole political process from the early 1990s onwards was to get out from under the shadow of communism, and that meant turning to the

West.[28]

However, as Viktor Orban of Hungary has been arguing so passionately over the last several years, Central and Eastern Europe are now experiencing their own European renaissance such that, while they don't necessarily disparage or want to bring down the EU, they certainly don't believe they are *dependent* on Brussels anymore. Indeed, Central and Eastern Europe are rediscovering that their cultures, customs, and traditions are absolutely essential for the revitalization of their national sovereignty. For example, for Bulgaria, this means rediscovering its Orthodox Christian tradition; back in the 1990's about 60 percent of Bulgarians identified themselves as Orthodox Christians, today it's over 75 percent. In fact, you have polls that indicate that the Orthodox Church is the single most trusted institution in Bulgaria.[29] And so, Central and Eastern Europe are rediscovering their culture, customs, and traditions as absolutely essential for the revitalization of their national sovereignty. And unfettered immigration, the kind being mandated by the quotas coming out of Brussels since 2015, is seen as inconsistent with just such a revitalization.

While Bulgaria is not a member of the Visegrad Four, Bulgaria has instituted virtually identical border security policies as those respective countries. Indeed, Prime minister Borissov, along with Viktor Orban of Hungary and Matteo Salvini of Italy, is calling for the EU to finance the border security for the front-line nations that are bearing a

---

[28] Lenka Buštíková, "The Radical Right in Eastern Europe," in Jens Rydgren (ed.), *The Oxford Handbook of the Radical Right* (Oxford: Oxford University Press, 2018), 565-81.
[29] http://orthochristian.com/101535.html.

disproportionate burden due to Merkel's open-ended invitation. And he's calling for processing centers and refugee camps to be set up outside of Europe, most likely in Northern African nations such as Algeria, Egypt, Libya, Morocco, Niger and Tunisia.

And it does appear that this is what they got out of the Summit. Nations like Hungary and Austria and Italy and Bulgaria went in wanting to leave the meeting with the absolute guarantee that the borders of Europe would be closed and secured with stringent security on the one hand, and a guarantee that the days of immigration quotas mandated from Brussels are over, guaranteeing that migrant camps would not be forced on any member nation in the EU. Those were the fundamental concessions that they wanted from Merkel; and got them they did.

And so, it does appear that the European Summit in late June is developing into a clear historical fixed point when we can look back and see how the European Union was transformed from a secular globalist super-state to looking more like a league of sovereign nations celebrating and indeed defending the cultural and traditional uniqueness of European civilization. When that transformation is complete, Europeans will have nations such as Bulgaria to thank.

CHAPTER 4

Matteo Salvini's Vision for a United Nationalist Europe

On the world's stage of nationalist leaders, few compare to the charm, whit, and indeed boldness of Matteo Salvini, the Deputy Prime Minister of Italy and leader of the nationalist right party, the League. When Salvini took over the leadership of what was then known as the Northern League (Lega Nord) back in 2013, it barely garnered five percent support among the Italian population; not only was the party consigned to the political fringe, it was corrupt and disorganized. And in a matter of just five years, Salvini took The League from a highly peripheral, disorganized political party and transformed it into one of the most popular, indeed one of the reigning parties in Italy, which is currently in a coalition government with the populist Five Star. There's little question that the League is one of the great political success stories in Europe.

Not long after taking office, Salvini gave a speech before the League's annual gathering just north of Milan, Salvini declared that the League was here to stay; indeed, he was confident that they would be governing Italy for the next 30 years! But such domestic political success appeared rather penultimate to Salvini, for he quickly turned his attention to the wider continent: "To win we had to unite Italy, now we will have to unite Europe," Salvini said. "I am thinking about a League of the Leagues of Europe, bringing together all the free and sovereign movements that want to defend their people and their borders."[30]

In many respects, Salvini has every reason to be confident and optimistic about such prospects. Domestically, the League received 17 percent of the vote in the March 4th, 2018 national election, as part of an overall center-right coalition that received a total of 37 percent of the vote. However, because the League got a higher percentage of the vote than did its coalition partner, the more 'mainstream' or center-right Forza Italia, supporters began to move away from Forza Italia and toward the League, seeing that the once fringe far-right party could now win elections. And so, since the national election in March, the League has nearly doubled their support to 30 percent. Moreover, candidates from the League dominated the mayoral elections held a few months later, demonstrating a political vibrancy at both the federal and local levels.

But internationally, such a success story among nationalist parties is not the League's alone. There are comparable political achievements in one nationalist populist party after another throughout Europe. Take, for example, the

---

[30] https://www.reuters.com/article/us-italy-politics-salvini-europe/italys-league-chief-salvini-vows-to-take-success-europe-wide-idUSKBN1JR1SI.

rise of the Sweden Democrats, which has been nothing short of stunning. In the 1980s and 1990s, they were barely getting over two or three percent support. But over time, they persuaded enough voters to first storm into parliament with about six percent of the vote in 2010, winning 20 seats. They then repeated their success four years later by doubling their support with 13 percent of the vote. They surged in support yet again with the recent 2018 elections, garnering 18 percent of the vote. Such trends suggest that the Sweden Democrats are well on their way to becoming the single biggest political party in Sweden.

There's no question, then, that the winds are at the backs of the nationalist right; and so Salvini's political success at the national level in Italy is being seen as a microcosm of the potential success of nationalist parties at the international macro level. In terms of bringing together the "free and sovereign movements," as he calls them, throughout the continent, Salvini is referring to the upcoming European Parliament elections in May of 2019. In view of those elections, Salvini is looking to build a dynamic network of nationalist parties around Europe to stand united in a single vision of a continent allied around democratic nationalist, populist, and traditionalist sentiments and commitments.

What Salvini is advocating here is but the latest chapter of a history of what scholars call the *internationalizing of the nationalist right*.[31] While leaders in the nationalist right

---

[31] Manuela Caiani, "Radical Right Cross-National Links and International Cooperation," in Jens Rydgren (ed.), *The Oxford*

have focused primarily on local and national elections, they all recognize that transnational politics are in many ways just as equally important, because the ultimate adversary in all of this is globalization, and globalization is by definition transnational. And so, virtually all of the national right organizations out there mobilize beyond just the national level, creating networks with likeminded organizations in other countries.

And so, we've seen organizations such as the European Alliance for Freedom emerge within the European Parliament, made up of the National Front, the Dutch Freedom Party, the Belgian Vlaams Belang, the Freedom Party of Austria, the Sweden Democrats, and the League. In addition, there was the Alliance of European Nationalist Movements founded back in 2009 that brought together the Jobbik party of Hungary, the Belgian National Front, the Finnish National Party, and others. Moreover, the nationalist right has often turned to non-political events that served as common networking sites, such as the heavy metal music festival Hammerfest which features a number of rightwing nationalist bands. Indeed, there are all kinds of ways for the nationalist right to create common networks and solidarity structures that bolster their common cause.

Moreover, Salvini's unifying vision of internationalizing the nationalist right involves clearly defining what Manuela Caiani calls *frames,* which are prerequisite to any macro-level cooperation. In this case, a frame involves clearly defined problems, goals, and solutions that different

Handbook of the Radical Right (Oxford: Oxford University Press, 2018), 394-411.

43

nations or national groups share in common, and so in such a way, frames form the basis of collective identities, including transnational and international ones, and thus provide the precondition for cooperation.[32] And as we've discussed above, the primary themes that coalesce together into unifying frames for creating cross-national links between the individual nationalist parties are border security, economic security, and cultural security. Studies of nationalist right pamphlets, websites, party newspapers, magazines, and the like have identified precisely these common issues that appear among virtually all nationalist right discourse. Virtually all of the rhetoric exemplifies a radical Euroskepticism (in the West; Eastern Europe is a bit more sympathetic to the EU), particularly against the insistence of Brussels to open the borders of Europe to Northern Africa and the Middle East; they are radically opposed to the globalizing processes that are replacing local economies, industries, and businesses with transnational corporations that have absolutely no loyalty to land, culture, or custom. And they stand steadfastly opposed to the multicultural assault on their nation, culture, and traditions particularly in light of the Islamization of Europe, which they see as the inevitable consequence of open borders globalization.

And so, in many respects, the themes behind the political platforms of the nationalist populist right throughout Europe have become identical; they want a united Europe, what they call a pan-European unity, but this unity must be

---

[32] Caiani, "Radical Right Cross-National Links," 396.

based on a diversity of distinct national identities rooted in a common classical and Christian civilization; they completely and unapologetically reject the contemporary technocracy of the European Union super state; they see globalization as an enemy common to all nations, cultures, and traditions; and they are banning together as one in a common fight against these dehumanizing dynamics and tendencies. Thus, the frames do appear to be there in order to bring about a united, transnational rightwing movement throughout the European continent. It's first test will certainly be the upcoming European Parliamentary elections in 2019, and if these trends behind the common frames are any indicator, we may very well see an election that changes the face of Europe forever.

CHAPTER 5

Denmark: The Triumph of a New Nationalist Paradigm

Denmark for decades has been what we might call the model nation for the social democrats, fulfilling the liberal ideals particularly of the Democratic Party in the United States. The Washington Post reported back in 2015 that Denmark was the single most cited model among the then-Democratic primary candidates for president, in that Denmark was famous for providing the most generous welfare benefits for their citizens, in terms of affordable education, universal healthcare, and subsidized child care.[33] In fact, no presidential candidate cited the example of Denmark more than Bernie Sanders, saying repeatedly that his vision of democratic socialism was best exemplified by countries like Denmark.

But that was during the primary season that began in 2015, before the refugee crisis that swamped Europe. Since then, Denmark is increasingly known for something else,

---

[33] https://www.washingtonpost.com/news/wonk/wp/2015/11/03/why-denmark-isnt-the-utopian-fantasy-bernie-sanders-describes/?utm_term=.4261091db950.

something very different than anything any liberal Democrat politically aspires to: Denmark has become one of the most 'far-right' nations in Europe as regards its immigration policies.

It's true; Denmark has recently become perhaps the single most dedicated nation to border security in Western Europe bar none. This was evident in a recent report published by a human rights NGO, the Global Detention Project, which was highly critical regarding the asylum and immigration practices in Denmark. This report accused Denmark of 'prison-like' asylum centers and the practice of detaining children in unsuitable facilities.[34]

Now given that the report was published by an NGO funded by far-left billionaire George Soros, it's impact on Denmark immigration policies is negligible. Nevertheless, the report is very informative, inadvertently of course, in terms of the window it provides into Denmark's immigration policies. The report notes that over the past three years, since the refugee crisis in 2015, Denmark has adopted just under 70 immigration-related amendments all of which have radically intensified border security and immigration restrictions. They've dramatically cut back on their asylum recognition rate, and they've called for detaining as many failed refugees as possible. And so, as a result, Denmark's rate of acceptance of asylum applications has plunged from 85 percent in 2015 to barely over 30 percent in 2017, and it's getting even more restrictive as we speak.

---

[34] https://www.globaldetentionproject.org/countries/europe/denmark.

So how did this happen in an otherwise social democratic paradise?

The short answer is that Denmark has experienced a mass political paradigm shift in the direction of the New Nationalism. Denmark's political parties, both traditionally left and right, are all vying to demonstrate to their voters that they are more conservative on border security they anyone else! In other words, border security and immigration is no longer a left or right issue; it has now officially and formally become *pre-political*; each political party is declaring the necessity of border security, and now it's just a matter of who's going to do it more effectively.

A political paradigm shift occurs when a once marginal or peripheral political policy or party moves from the margins to the mainstream; there is a movement away from the political fringe and toward the direction of becoming the consensus opinion among a population. And when it comes to border security and national sovereignty, Denmark has rejected the globalist vision of the European Union and its open borders, and instead has shifted in mass to the nationalist populist right.

We should not overlook the role of the so-called 'far-right' Danish People's Party, the Dansk Folkeparti (DF), in initiating this paradigm shift. The DF is the second-most popular party in Denmark and at the center of its ruling rightwing coalition. They are in fact one of the most successful rightwing parties in Europe, having been able to significantly shape domestic policy in Denmark, at the heart of which is a very strict border security policy.

But their success has gone beyond merely influencing the politics and platform of the Danish right. Reports have been coming out of late that recognize that even the traditionally left-wing parties are turning increasingly towards the right when it comes to immigration. A relatively recent headline from Bloomberg says it well: "Danish Leftists Turn on Migrants in Bid to Regain Power."[35] In fact, the center-left Social Democrats in Denmark have already declared that they will not form a coalition with any other leftist party in Denmark. As traditionally the center-left party, the Social Democrats are currently the largest single party in the Danish parliament, but the rightwing coalition holds the overall majority. And for the past 25 years, the Social Democrats have caucused with the other leftwing parties in Denmark, but no longer. The whole issue of immigration has turned Denmark's center-left towards the nationalist right in policy and platform.

We need to understand that with the rise of the New Nationalism, the whole issue of traditional left and right is blurring; in many ways, it's collapsing. While issues such as taxes, regulation, and governmental centralization remain important, they're no longer central to the political debate. At issue today is increasingly a paradigmatic debate over whether we're going to embrace globalism or nationalism; are we going to have open borders or are we going to secure our borders; are we going to be a multicultural society or are we going to embrace our cultural, traditional, and religious uniqueness and identity? *This* is the new political

---

[35] https://www.bloomberg.com/news/articles/2017-05-08/jewelry-scandal-shows-path-to-power-as-danes-redefine-socialism

paradigm emerging throughout the world, and it is the nationalist, populist, and traditionalist right that is directing and often winning this mass paradigm shift. And Denmark and the other Nordic nations, such as Norway and Finland, are no exception. Indeed, if anything, Denmark in many respects is leading the way.

With the rise of the New Nationalism, the global political order is changing dramatically. Nations once considered ideal bastions of secular liberalism are recalibrating around immigration policies once associated solely with the radical right. And so, perhaps the best evidence for this paradigm shift is that for the first time, conservative nationalists can all agree with the conclusions of leftist liberal Democrats: Denmark truly is a model nation.

CHAPTER 6

The Prince of Nationalists: Vladimir Putin and the Russian Renewal

By the time Vladimir Putin won his fourth-term as president of the Russian Federation, he had already been the longest serving leader of Russia since Stalin, serving as president for the previous 14 years.[36] If we include his time as prime-minister, by the end of Putin's fourth-term, he will have ruled Russia for over two decades.

To the disappointment of Western elites and Eurocrats alike, Vladimir Putin remains extremely popular among the Russian population. For example, survey after survey indicates that young people in Russia are the single most pro-Putin element within the Russian population. They're also the most patriotic, the most nationalist of Russians, as well as the most optimistic for their nation's future. Just prior to the 2018 presidential election in Russia, *The Washington Post* published statistics showing that 81 percent of Russians approved of Putin as President; for

---

[36] The presidency of Russia was extended from a four-year term to a six-year term during Dmitry Medvedev's administration back in 2008.

those between the ages of 18 and 24, that number rose to 86 percent. 67 percent of young people believed the country was headed in the right direction, along with 56 percent of the population over all.

How did Putin achieve such incredible popularity? Well, I don't think it's a matter of Putin intimidating and threatening his way to the top through Stalin-like fear, as we so often hear from our Western elite, who seem to never tire of accusing Putin of killing off everyone who disagrees with him. Paul Robinson, a Canadian professor in Russian studies who blogs over at Irrusianality.com, has documented how more journalists and political dissidents were killed under Boris Yeltsin's tenure than Putin's administrations, ironically enough, due largely to the breakdown of law and order after the fall of the Soviet Union. So, I must admit that I do tend to give Putin the benefit of the doubt for the most part.

Nevertheless, with the last presidential election, polls and surveys have been confirmed: Vladimir Putin remains a very, very popular president among the Russian population. So why is that?

I would argue that it's because since the turn of the 21st century, President Putin has successfully brought Russia out of the bewildering, confusing fallout from the implosion of the Soviet Union. Keep in mind that after the collapse of communism, everything Russians had been taught to believe as absolute truth for seven decades quite literally imploded overnight, exposed as nothing more than a totalitarian and genocidal lie. And in the midst of this wreckage, Vladimir Putin gave Russians the opportunity to rediscover their traditional heritage, faith, culture, and religion as a revived metanarrative that could lead them into a flourishing and prosperous future.

What we have to remember is that with the collapse of the Soviet Union on Christmas of 1991, Russia lost its unifying metanarrative: the communist vision of dialectical materialism, the belief that the capitalist vision of the world was doomed to failure and an inevitable global communist utopia was the end of history, this belief fell apart, and the Russian world suddenly found itself devoid of any ideological or cultural glue to hold its society together. Boris Yeltsin attempted a Western-inspired civic Russian identity, rooted in a new commitment to democratic freedoms and statehood, but that faltered about as quickly as it started; there just wasn't any real moral foundation that could sustain this globalist metanarrative of unending progress and free markets and liberal democracy and human rights.

But then, Vladimir Putin came to power, and as the Russian philosopher Aleksandr Dugin has written about,[37] Putin recognized that Russia had to rediscover a compelling metanarrative that could bind the nation together into a single, unified civilization once again. With communism dead, something even more compelling, more deeply rooted in the Russian soul would have to take its place. And *that* is the real contribution of Vladimir Putin; he found that the way forward for Russians would be a return, a retraditionalization that would involve reawakening

---

[37] Aleksandr Dugin, *Putin vs. Putin: Vladimir Putin Viewed from the Right* (Arktos Media Ltd, 2014).

Russia's pre-Soviet history, her culture, traditions, customs, and Orthodox religion that would serve as the foundation for a rebirth and renewal of Russian civilization.

In many respects, since the fall of the Soviet Union, what we know as the Russian Federation was ready to almost completely split part. Although Russia remains primarily Russian (about 78 percent of the population are still ethnic Russians), still it's a nation that has over 190 nationalities. And so, while predominantly ethnically Russian, the federation remains very densely multi-ethnic. And this of course has been a point of contention within Russian society, particularly after the fall of communism. The Baltic nations were the first to assert their national sovereignty with the collapse of the Soviet Union. And so, Russia was faced with the prospect of more and more multi-ethnic factions and enclaves breaking away from the Federation.

The answer for Vladimir Putin was to re-envision the nation of Russia as a 'multinational nation,' which is a distinct vision of Russian nationalism. What we hear throughout Putin's speeches is the notion that Russian culture is a gift to the world; Russian literature, art, music, Orthodoxy, customs, and traditions, and Russian heroism and protection of peoples and nations, this is a gift to the world. Russia is a culture that is a divine gift for all peoples, nations, customs, and traditions; and therefore, by definition, Russian culture is multi-ethnic. The notion that Russia is a gift to the world necessitates the free participation of other nationalities. This seems to me to be key to Putin's nationalist project; Russia by its nature is a multinational nation; Russian culture is a gift to the world, and thus by definition requires the participation of multiple nations and ethnicities.

It is here that we can see why Putin would be so problematic for the globalist world order. Putin does not celebrate a secularized vision of human rights irrespective of culture; he doesn't affirm a notion of civil rights that favors certain races, genders, and sexual orientations. Rather, the rights, protections, and freedoms experienced by citizens of the Russian Federation are the direct result of a distinctively Russian culture, religion, society, and sentiments. *This* is the key difference between the New Nationalism that's rising all over the world and the neo-conservative/neo-liberal center-right/center-left globalist politics that have dominated the world stage since the early 1990s. With the end of the Soviet Union, the political language that dominated the geo-political scene was reflective of a one-size-fits-all political, economic, and cultural system for all peoples, times and places. Liberal democracy, corporate-based free markets, human rights, and lifestyle values, these were the supposed new norms for every single nation on the earth; specific cultures, religions, races, customs, traditions, histories, languages, and ways of life suddenly became irrelevant, indeed subservient, to a globalist set of political, economic, and cultural standards and protocols. That's why religion is irrelevant to the European Union; it's why culture, custom, and tradition are irrelevant to a globalist world order. Indeed, cultures, customs, and traditions are not merely irrelevant, they're increasingly denounced and rejected as homophobic, racist, xenophobic, nativist, and bigoted.

However, for Putin's vision of a multi-national nation, the emphasis on culturally-derived freedoms *necessitates* a commitment to traditional values, since traditionalist values protect and perpetuate the culture. Because the center-right or center-left coalitions focus on individual rights, traditions and customs are often viewed as impediments to social justice and are thus re-branded as bigoted and exclusionary. A multinational nation – as Putin calls it – requires traditionalist values to protect and maintain the culture that's the source for the rights and freedoms experienced by its citizens and its multiple micro-cultures and ethnicities.

It is here that the Russian Orthodox Church has played perhaps the most significant role in the Russian nationalist renewal. If Putin's multi-national Russia by definition requires traditionalist values to maintain and protect it, then there has to be a cultural source for those traditionalist values, and that is the role of the Russian Orthodox Church. According to the study by the church historian John Burgess, the Russian Orthodox Church is occupying a moral and ideational role in the life of Russia comparable to that once played by Soviet communism.[38]

This moral foundation, interestingly enough, is the way in which Russia avoids collapsing into multiculturalism. Both President Putin and Patriarch Kirill warn of the harmful effects of multiculturalism, which they see as destroying the majority culture in favor of absolutizing minority cultures through civil rights which inevitably end up

---

[38] John P. Burgess, *Holy Rus': The Rebirth of Orthodoxy in the New Russia* (New Haven: Yale University Press, 2017).

clashing with one another, since there's no meta-culture that serves as their common ground. There's no metanarrative to sustain multicultural societies; whatever metanarrative might be put forward will eventually be rejected by one of the minority cultures; which of course is what we're seeing here in the States and throughout Western Europe.

And so, what we've seen emerge from Russia over the course of nearly two decades is nothing less than a new metanarrative that's replaced the old communist one; the new post-Soviet Russia is a return to Holy Rus, traditional Russia, where Russian culture, religion, and society offer to the world a very particular way of being human that invites all nations, cultures, and traditions into itself for a flourishing and prosperous future. It is precisely the success of that metanarrative that I believe is ultimately behind the astonishing success of Vladimir Putin.

CHAPTER 7

Turkey: A New Islamic Republic

A massive political earthquake hit Turkey on April 16, 2017, but not one that shook the ground. Instead, a referendum was (narrowly) approved that involved 18 constitutional amendments, one of which, perhaps most significantly, included the abolition of the office of prime minister, which was subsequently nullified in July of 2018. Many believe that the abolition of the position of prime minister will have the effect of eliminating a critical counterbalance to President Recep Tayyip Erdoğan's power, which according to the referendum, will continue unabated now until the year 2029.

However, what is a clear consequence of this referendum is the end of *secular* Turkey; indeed, in many respects, the reigning secular paradigm that has defined Turkey since its founding in 1923 has all but imploded. Turkey is moving increasingly toward traditional Islamic societal and political norms, and for a number of reasons.

First, while Turkey has prided itself as a secular nation, particularly upheld and guarded by the military as stipulated by its constitution, this secularism has always been rather tenuous. We have to remember that secularism was never the ideology of the masses; it was imposed on Turks from an elite aristocracy – both intellectual elite as well as military elite – imposed from above, largely inspired by Western social and cultural norms. One writer put it this way: "Modern Turkey is a strange amalgam of Western structures underpinned by Ottoman habits."[39] That's a great description. Kemalism, which was the secular reforms imposed by Turkey's original leader, Kemal Atatürk, involved such extremes as introducing a Latin-based alphabet which cut Turks off from their Arabic literary traditions to banning traditional forms of attire. So, this secular society was always in many respects a thoroughly aristocratic and elitist invention.

Now with the rise of a Brexit-like blowback going on all over the world, Turkey too has begun to see its society in terms of a secularized globalist elite on the one hand and traditionalist conservative Muslims on the other. Over the last several years we've seen the rise of traditionalist conservatives in the political realm, which is progressively and dramatically reshaping Turkish society and culture. For example, since the early 1980s, much of the national educational system has been Islamized; education prior to the 1980s tended to downplay the Ottoman Empire and encultured students to think of secularism as progressive and enlightened. But since the Islamization of much of the educational system, the Ottoman Empire was taught as an

---

[39] http://katehon.com/article/russia-and-turkey-consistency-versus-unreliability.

ideal society filled with enriching Islamic culture that is itself the wave of the future. That is how the majority of the nation has been educated over the last few decades.

We also have to remember that after the failed coup attempt back in July of 2016, many of the secularist remnant have been, shall we say, cleansed by Erdogan's rather brutal response. As it turns out, Kemalist military-based secularism was just simply unsustainable; it never seemed to seep into the hearts and minds of the majority of Turkish citizens. And the climax of this nationalist traditionalist wave seems to be the passing of the referendum, however slim the margin.

Regardless, a number of scholars have noted that both Erdogan and his party, the AKP or Justice and Development Party, are interested in transforming Turkey more into a neo-Anatolian federation of Muslim ethnicities rather than a secular democratic republic of Turkish citizens, and this transformation may even involve a revived caliphate.[40]

What this means is that Turkey is moving away from the Western European model of liberal democracy and towards a far more traditionalist conservative culture and social order, which, as we've seen above, is an identifiable worldwide trend. Nations are more and more turning away from the anti-cultural, anti-religious dynamics of secular globalism and instead turning towards those cultural and religious frames of reference that constitute their historic national identities. So, I think that this shift towards the

---

[40] https://www.military.com/daily-news/2018/03/13/op-ed-erdogan-magnificent-turkeys-neo-ottoman-revival.html.

more traditionalist conservative vision of faith and life that's going on at a global level is the main reason why secularism has imploded in Turkey.

The second reason is that Erdogan recently did an about face toward Russia, and it appears inevitable that an Islamic-based Turkey is going to find far more common ground with traditionalist-based Orthodox Russia than with NATO or the highly secularized European Union. There's nothing that Russia would like more than to weaken NATO and eventually bring Turkey under its sphere of Eurasian influence. And this likelihood of a Russo-Turkish alliance is all the more exacerbated by – you guessed it – Western secularism: the more the West adopts feminist, homosexual, and transgender policies, the more the West alienates itself away from traditionalist and conservative social orders. And it is certainly doing that with Turkey. Now as Ankara is re-envisioning itself as the center of a neo-Ottoman empire, so Moscow is re-envisioning itself as the center of a neo-Byzantium empire. And in many respects, there are thinkers who see both Russia and the Ottoman Empires as the joint heirs of Byzantium, and therefore there is a very real possibility and a highly romantic one of a Russo-Turkish, anti-Western and anti-liberal alliance.

Now regardless of exactly how it turns out, it does appear that the passage of the referendum certainly favors a resurgence of neo-Ottoman sensibilities in the hearts and minds of Turks throughout the nation, and with such, it does appear that we are seeing nothing less than the implosion of secularism in Turkey. And this implosion factors further in the collapse of secularism throughout the Western world. We're not just seeing the death of secular globalism in Russia and Eastern Europe as well as Poland and Slovakia, but we are seeing the demise of secularism in the US as well. We are witnessing the increasing collapse of multiculturalism and political correctness. On the one hand, a hardline anti-immigration policy proposal – once considered the political death knell for a Republican candidate – won overwhelmingly at the ballot box in the 2016 election and continues to be more popular than ever. On the other hand, multiculturalism is morphing into tribalization and balkanization on the political left. The Black Lives Matter movement, for example, is nothing less than an ethno-nationalist movement, a kind of absolutist tribalization that rejects secular notions of tolerance and inclusivity. Secular multicultural and tolerance norms are collapsing all over the place, not merely due to the wave of nationalist populist sentiments on the right, but also due to the split allegiances that occur as the result of multiculturalism.

So, it does appear that globalist secular liberalism is in fact collapsing all over the globe, and the Turkish referendum is only the latest and perhaps most explicit example of secularism's slow but inevitable demise.

CHAPTER 8

India and the Rise of Hindu Nationalism

Nationalism, particularly in its retraditionalized and religious form, is literally flooding India. Indeed, the rise of Hindu nationalism in what was once a self-professed secular nation has much to tell us about the nationalist populist surge going on throughout the world.

Back in 2014, the Bharatiya Janata Party, which is the right-wing party of India, won the single largest democratic election in human history. The Bharatiya Janata Party of India, or BJP, is far and away the largest political party in the world, and it is a thoroughly nationalist, populist, and most especially, traditionalist political party. In turn, the BJP became the leading party of the largest and most diverse democracy in the world and is overwhelmingly poised to win the upcoming 2019 national elections. It is therefore no exaggeration to predict that this right-wing party will be defining the political landscape in India for years to come.

At the heart of the BJP and its electoral success is its leader and the current prime-minister, Narendra Modi. Prime Minister Modi comes from thoroughly right-wing Hindu nationalist corners; he was part of an organization called the Rashtriya Swayamsevak Sangh, or RSS, which is a Hindu nationalist group that explicitly seeks to reorganize the Indian nation, society, and culture around conservative Hindu beliefs and practices, or Hindutva. The RSS is considered the intellectual and social foundation of the BJP, the current ruling party in India.

Modi ran on a thoroughly nationalist and populist platform; he was firmly anti-establishment, anti-elite, and led a mass electoral rebellion against the center-left Indian National Congress Party, which is basically the secular globalist party in India. Interestingly, as a politician, Modi's right up there with our own President Donald Trump; in fact, he's the second most followed world leader on Twitter next to Trump.

And under his tenure, India has moved radically to the Hindu nationalist right. For example, the Indian public-school system is more and more adopting Hindutva or a distinctively Hindu nationalist curriculum that involves prayers and hymns devoted to Hindu gods throughout the school day.[41] The BJP has pushed for changing the names of Muslim streets to replace them with names less offensive to Hindu nationalists. The party has changed Muslim names in textbooks, replacing them with Hindu versions of their names. And the BJP has forced colleges to cancel speaker invitations to anti-nationalist activists and demonstrators.

---

[41] https://www.huffingtonpost.in/2017/09/18/in-rss-schools-muslims-students-are-learning-to-live-with-hindutva_a_23155028/.

Now obviously there have been many parallels drawn between Prime Minister Modi and President Trump. They've been described as kindred spirits, both of whom are committed nationalists and willing to forego the niceties of the political elites in both countries to get things done on behalf of a population eager for more jobs and economic growth. Modi is definitely an 'India First' leader and proponent of economic nationalism and protectionism. Trump's populist politics and his claim that "a nation without borders is not a nation," really resonates in India just as it is resonating throughout the world. We can see virtually identical nationalist populist rhetoric coming from Modi, Trump, Nigel Farage of Brexit fame, France's Marine Le Pen, the young Sebastian Kurz of Austria, and the new prime minister of the Czech Republic, Andrej Babis, who's affectionally known as the Czech Trump.

The Hindu nationalist project got a huge boost with the recent election of Ram Nath Kovind for president of India. Ram Nath Kovind was backed by Modi and the BJP, and he won a landslide victory with 65 percent of the vote. So, now the BJP occupy the prime-minister, president, and vice-president as well as the majority of the lower house in India's bicameral system. Only the upper house stands in the way of a full BJP dominance over Indian governance, and that opposition will most likely be swept away in the upcoming elections if past trajectories hold up.

Thus, what we are seeing in India is in many respects perhaps the single most startling example of what we've been calling retraditionalization going on in a nation outside of the likes of Russia, Hungary, Poland, and

Bulgaria. Because globalization entails secularizing processes that challenge the traditions, customs, and religions of local cultures, its processes tend to be resisted with a counter-cultural blowback. In the face of threats to localized identity markers, populations are increasingly asserting their religiosity, kinship, and national symbols as mechanisms of resistance against globalizing dynamics.

India was long touted as the ideal secular nation. In one sense, at the popular level, it was thoroughly religious; in fact, scholars have longed argued that India is constituted by the most religious population on the planet. But in its government and education system and standards of civil rights, India considered itself to be thoroughly secular, neither favoring nor discriminating against any particular religion. This very idealist conception of secularism has waned in recent years, not just in India but throughout the world. And like we noted above with Erdogan's Turkey, in many respects, secularism was a European enlightenment idea imposed on India's population from the top down. The population as a whole was never actually secularized, and thus, it was just a matter of time before the illusion of secularism as an enlightened and just and religiously-neutral political system came crashing down. And that seems to have been the case in India. Secularism is more and more seen as involving a politically leftist bent that was more and more interpreted as being anti-Hindu and therefore thoroughly anti-Indian. Secularism became increasingly identified with an out-of-touch political, educational, and media elite that had little to do with the population as a whole.

And so, India, under the leadership of Prime Minister Modi, has in fact emerged as a thoroughly post-secular nation, very similar to Turkey, Russia, Poland, and Hungary. Of course, a number of Western commentators are lamenting this development, especially in terms of how the rise of a retraditionalized nationalist populism involves the political persecution of minority religions. For example, there have been reports of forced conversion attempts on Christian families in Indian villages by Hindu nationalists, the desecration of churches, and actual physical violence and assaults against Christians, Muslims, and Buddhists. These are of course unacceptable in any humane society.

But what we have to understand is that, unfortunately, such acts of religious persecution are really just par for the course given the fact that secularism is seen more and more as that ideology that persecutes a nation's dominant religious identity. Remember, what's fueling the retraditionalization that's going on all over the world is a response or blowback to an overwhelming sense of threat, wherein the very survival of key identity markers of a people and nation – such as religion, culture, custom, tradition, land, ethnicity, language, history – are all viewed as imperiled. To just defer to good ol' fashioned secular human rights such as religious freedom, as our Western elites like to do, does absolutely nothing to remedy this problem, but I believe has the reverse effect; it employs rhetoric that only exasperates it.

Regardless, given domestic and worldwide currents, we can safely predict that India will continue to blossom as a post-secular nation, and continue to foster a thoroughly Hindu nationalist culture that is itself a bellwether on upcoming right-wing nationalist turns throughout the world.

CHAPTER 9

President Donald Trump: Making America Great Again

"A new chapter of American greatness is now beginning."

So said President Donald Trump in his first speech to the joint session of the United States congress in February of 2017.[42] It was by virtually all accounts a magnificent speech, acknowledged by both sides of the aisle. But for our purposes, it is an excellent example of the nationalist populist frames of reference that are informing the New Nationalism throughout the world, albeit in a distinctively American context. Thus, in what follows, I want to analyze the speech in light of these themes and, in so doing, appreciate why the political philosophy that Trump laid out in his agenda is a thoroughly coherent vision of a new political world order.

---

[42] The full speech can be accessed at:
https://www.whitehouse.gov/briefings-statements/remarks-president-trump-joint-address-congress/.

The interpretive grid through which I'm reading Trump's speech comes from the then-White House Chief Strategist, Steve Bannon. During the week prior to the speech, Bannon laid out the grand strategy of Trump's governing philosophy at the Conservative Political Action Conference or CPAC, a strategy that he assisted in developing, where he delineated what he called the 'three verticals' of Trump's new political order: economic nationalism, national sovereignty, and the deconstruction of the administrative state.[43] Below I shall read Trump's speech in many ways as organized around precisely these three verticals.

Economic Nationalism

First, Trump spelled out explicitly his program of economic nationalism. He talked about clearing the way for the construction of the Keystone and Dakota Access Pipelines, which will involve creating tens of thousands of jobs, but of course with the caveat that the pipelines had to be made with American steel. It will be built by Americans with American industry and American material.

President Trump then went on to list out the manufacturing casualties of NAFTA, where we've lost some 60,000 factories in the last 15 years. Here Trump may in fact have been influenced by Bannon, who sees urbanization as intrinsic to globalization, such that the manufacturing jobs constitutive of employment in the rustbelt areas in places such as Wisconsin, Iowa, Michigan, and Pennsylvania are

---

[43] A transcript of Bannon's talk/interview at:
http://time.com/4681094/reince-priebus-steve-bannon-cpac-interview-transcript/.

farmed out to Mexico and China by the financial sectors comprised of corporatist globalists working in places like Los Angeles County and Manhattan. This is why Bannon sees the populist movement in America as primarily a blue-collar rural uprising against white collar corporatist urbanites. And this is also why Bannon and Trump see the rustbelt areas of the country as essential to the realignment of the GOP around this mass new demographic of disaffected voters, since the Democrats have largely lost them due to the left's devotion to urbanized gentry liberal values and identity politics.

Trump then recalled a conversation he had with workers from Harley-Davidson, and Trump asked them how their business was going. They said it was good, and he further asked the how they were doing with other countries, with international sales. And without complaining, they did express their frustration with being mistreated by other countries, some of which were taxing their motorcycles at 100 percent. And then Trump looked out at the chambers and said: "They weren't even asking for change. But I am!" Here Trump established himself as the populist representative, the advocate of the American worker and, in so doing, most likely secured every vote from virtually every employee of Harley-Davidson.

He then went on to talk about infrastructure spending in the US. He noted that we've spent over six trillion dollars in the Middle East all the while infrastructure here at home is crumbling. He surmised as he does so often at his stump speeches and rallies that with six trillion dollars, we could have rebuilt our country two or three times over. Again, note the globalist (Middle East)/nationalist (here at home) contrast. It is in this context that Trump asked congress for $1 trillion in infrastructure spending that will be financed both through public and private capital, creating millions of new jobs that will be guided by two core principles: "Buy American and Hire American."

In many ways, this was Steve Bannon's economic nationalism coming out throughout the speech which appeals to blue collar voters particularly in the rust belt states of Wisconsin, Iowa, Michigan, and Pennsylvania, all of which Trump won in 2016 and without which no Democrat will ever win the White House again. And someone like the ultra-liberal Van Jones recognized this: if the GOP is effective in this political realignment, it's a pretty dire future for Democrats.

National Sovereignty and Border Security

Then Trump moved on to the second plank of this new political order: national sovereignty and security. Here of course Trump pushed the building of a great wall that will keep drugs and thugs out of the US. And he further made it clear that he is committed to actually enforcing the illegal immigration laws that are already on the books. Trump stated that he was committed to stomping out radical Islamic terrorism and working with our allies in NATO to do just that. And as part of this strategy, he renewed his commitment to extreme vetting of immigrants from nations that do not have adequate vetting protocols or procedures.

Trump then went on to announce the development of a new Department of Homeland Security organization called VOICE, Victims Of Immigration Crime Engagement, which will provide a voice for those ignored by the globalist media and silenced by pro-amnesty special interests. He then introduced four family members of victims murdered by illegal immigrants, again all to underscore his commitment to our national sovereignty and security.

And immigration and economic nationalism came together in his proposal for a merit-based immigration system, like they have in Canada and Australia, where those entering into the country ought to be able to support themselves financially. There's no reason why immigration should include those who can't provide for themselves and who then go on welfare programs paid for by the American worker. This is Trump's form of welfare chauvinism, which has become a hallmark in the political platforms of the New Nationalists in Europe; welfare is for the citizens of a nation only, and not free for the taking for anyone who happens to cross over the border.

Trump then affirmed that American sovereignty means a multi-polar world where the sovereignty of other nations will be honored by the US. He wants harmony and stability with other nations, not war and conflict. But a multi-polar world of democratic nations will happen only in the context of turning our backs on globalism, as Trump made clear: "My job is not to represent the world. My job is to represent the United States of America." He is an America First president. It is this commitment to national sovereignty that protects and perpetuates economic nationalism.

Deconstruction of the Administrative State

At the CPAC conference the week before Trump's speech to congress, Bannon talked about what he called the 'deconstruction of the administrative state.' Now, by 'administrative state' he is referring to what is the term *du jour* for the permanent bureaucracy which has been almost completely amputated from any constitutional oversight. And here Trump of course brought up repealing and replacing the disaster of Obamacare, and laid out five principles that should guide Congress in such a process, such as taking care of everyone who has pre-existing conditions; the America First political order involves taking care of all citizens such that no one should be knocked off coverage who can't get it any other way; making healthcare more accessible through expanding tax credits and Health Savings Accounts; and giving Americans the freedom to purchase health insurance across state lines which promises to drive down costs while raising value.

Trump talked about slashing regulations and restraints particularly with the Food and Drug Administration and on businesses. He spoke of disestablishing the US Department of Education by instituting a national school choice initiative and tax credit scholarship program; and he announced that he has put together an economic team that is developing historic tax reform and reduction.

Summary: Making America and the World Great Again

Trump's first speech to the joint session of congress laid out a thoroughly coherent nationalist populist agenda, comprised of economic nationalism, national sovereignty and border security, and the dismantling of the administrative state. As regards particularly his economic and nationalist themes, Trump's vision for restoring America's sovereignty away from decades of globalized economic and demographic affects resonates well with the concerns of the New Nationalism that we've seen throughout the world. It is this New Nationalism that provides a coherent political philosophy which represents nothing less than a new political order, the influence of which is only just beginning.

Thank you again for purchasing this book!

I hope this book encouraged you by showing you all the ways the world is becoming more nationalist, populist, and traditionalist.

If you enjoyed this book, then I'd like to ask you for a favor: Would you be kind enough to leave a review for this book on Amazon? I would so greatly appreciate it!

Thank you so much, and may God richly bless you!

Steve Turley

www.turleytalks.com

Check Out My Other Books

Below you'll find some of my other popular books that are popular on Amazon. Simply go to the links below to check them out. Alternatively, you can visit my author page on Amazon to see my other works.

- *The Triumph of Tradition: How the Resurgence of Religion is Reawakening a Conservative World* https://amzn.to/2xieNO3

- *Classical vs. Modern Education: A Vision from C.S. Lewis* http://amzn.to/2opDZju

- *President Trump and Our Post-Secular Future: How the 2016 Election Signals the Dawning of a Conservative Nationalist Age* http://amzn.to/2B87Q22

- *Gazing: Encountering the Mystery of Art* https://amzn.to/2yKi6k9

- *Beauty Matters: Creating a High Aesthetic in School Culture* https://amzn.to/2L8Ejd7

- *Ever After: How to Overcome Cynical Students with the Role of Wonder in Education* http://amzn.to/2jbJI78

- *Movies and the Moral Imagination: Finding Paradise in Films* http://amzn.to/2zjghJj

- *Health Care Sharing Ministries: How Christians are Revolutionizing Medical Cost and Care* http://amzn.to/2B2Q8B2

- *The Face of Infinite of Love: Athanasius on the Incarnation* http://amzn.to/2oxULNM

- *Stressed Out: Learn How an Ancient Christian Practice Can Relieve Stress and Overcome Anxiety* http://amzn.to/2kFzcpc

- *Wise Choice: Six Steps to Godly Decision Making* http://amzn.to/2qy3C2Z

- *Awakening Wonder: A Classical Guide to Truth, Goodness, and Beauty* http://amzn.to/2ziKR5H

- *Worldview Guide for* A Christmas Carol http://amzn.to/2BCcKHO

- *The Ritualized Revelation of the Messianic Age: Washings and Meals in Galatians and 1 Corinthians* http://amzn.to/2B0mGvf

If the links do not work, for whatever reason, you can simply search for these titles on the Amazon website to find them.

About www.TurleyTalks.com

Are we seeing the revitalization of Christian civilization?

For decades, the world has been dominated by a process known as globalization, an economic and political system that hollows out and erodes a culture's traditions, customs, and religions, all the while conditioning populations to rely on the expertise of a tiny class of technocrats for every aspect of their social and economic lives.

Until now.

All over the world, there's been a massive blowback against the anti-cultural processes of globalization and its secular aristocracy. From Russia to Europe and now in the U.S., citizens are rising up and reasserting their religion, culture, and nation as mechanisms of resistance against the dehumanizing tendencies of secularism and globalism.

And it's just the beginning.

The secular world is at its brink, and a new traditionalist age is rising.

Join me each week as we examine these worldwide trends, discover answers to today's toughest challenges, and together learn to live in the present in light of even better things to come.

So hop on over to www.TurleyTalks.com and have a look around. Make sure to sign-up for our weekly Email Newsletter where you'll get lots of free giveaways, private Q&As, and tons of great content. Check out our YouTube channel (www.youtube.com/c/DrSteveTurley) where you'll understand current events in light of conservative trends to help you flourish in your personal and professional life. And of course, 'Like' us on Facebook and follow us on Twitter.

Thank you so much for your support and for your part in this cultural renewal.

About the Author

Steve Turley (PhD, Durham University) is an internationally recognized scholar, speaker, and classical guitarist. He is the author of over a dozen books, including *Classical vs. Modern Education: A Vision from C.S. Lewis, Awakening Wonder: A Classical Guide to Truth, Goodness, and Beauty*, and *The Ritualized Revelation of the Messianic Age: Washings and Meals in Galatians and 1 Corinthians*. Steve's popular YouTube channel showcases weekly his expertise in the rise of nationalism, populism, and traditionalism throughout the world, and his podcasts and writings on civilization, society, culture, education, and the arts are widely accessed at TurleyTalks.com. He is a faculty member at Tall Oaks Classical School in Bear, DE, where he teaches Theology and Rhetoric, and Professor of Fine Arts at Eastern University. Steve lectures at universities, conferences, and churches throughout the U.S. and abroad. His research and writings have appeared in such journals as *Christianity and Literature, Calvin Theological Journal, First Things, Touchstone*, and *The Chesterton Review*. He and his wife, Akiko, have four children and live in Newark, DE, where they together enjoy fishing, gardening, and watching *Duck Dynasty* marathons.

Made in the USA
Columbia, SC
24 July 2019